Survival Preparedness

A Beginners Guide to Survival Prepping

Published in the United States of America by
BestSurvivalKnifeDude.com.

First Edition

Disclaimer

Any content and information within this book is for informational and educational purposes only and any use thereof is solely at your own risk.

No part of this book may be reproduced or transmitted in any form without explicit written permission from the author. Excerpts of the book may be used for the purposes of review.

This book is dedicated to my loving wife and kids. Thank you for your support. – Love Kenneth

Great Reviews are Very Helpful

If you find the content within this book helpful, please leave a positive review. As you will learn within this book, survival preparedness is a critical component of caring for your family.

If this book has been helpful, please go to Amazon.com and let the other potential readers know what you think about the book. For your convenience, you can leave a review using the link below.

https://www.amazon.com/review/create-review?ie=UTF8&asin=B00O5C4CS0

Table of Contents

Survival Preparedness

In today's time, a handful of threats could make you fearful of the future. Aside from the war that's going on, there are various things to be worried about: the widespread of mysterious diseases, economic downfalls and calamities brought about by environmental negligence. Most of which are showcased on the television, making you feel even more afraid of what's going to happen next. These inevitable turns of events pose a threat to your safety and security, which are more than enough to make you feel anxious.

Being prepared is essential. The sooner you are, the safer and more secure you will feel. This survival preparedness plan is your aid in getting ready for the inevitable. This book includes information on:

- Emergency evacuation for tragedies including fire, flood, hurricane and non-environmental accidents.
- Ease and comfort during quarantine or isolation periods.
- Outages or interruptions for water and electricity that

may sometimes last for days and even weeks.

- Preparing for biological or chemical threats during terrorist attacks.

- Long term unemployment security, compensation enough to live comfortable life.

Disaster strikes when you least expect it and God only knows when that will be. What you do know is you are bound to meet disaster along the way. If you have prepared enough though, you will likely experience less anxiety and panic.

To be prepared and secured for the future, be it long-term or short-term, there are several things that you can do. Following the suggestions below will ease your worries and provide a peaceful sleep at night during chaotic times.

Short-Term: The 72-Hour Emergency Kit

For short-term preparedness, the 72-Hour Emergency Kit can do just the job. It is a portable kit that is intended to help you get through a natural disaster or any form of emergency that traps you outdoors. Items included in this are those that you can easily grab and go, and place them conveniently in a back pack.

A short-term kit's purpose is basically limited to sustaining your basic needs while in search for a safe location or a shelter to settle. Intended for periods where help is still on its way or is not yet within your reach, the kit contains items that can be utilized while on the move. This is pretty much like a survival kit that you would bring with you when going on a hike.

A Long-Term Supply of Food and Water

Most emergency cases only last short-term, but it is inevitable that the aftermath of some disasters would take you more than three weeks to recover. Major calamities would require you to be fully equipped for months following an emergency.

* * *

Fighting over food supplies at the grocery store surely isn't what you would want to do when emergency strikes. It would cause you more discomfort and danger than what you are already experiencing. That is why a year's worth of food will prove to be helpful in some cases.

However, this scenario is not just limited to calamities; another situation that you need to prepare for may come in a form of a major financial breakdown. Getting laid off from your job due to recession might cause serious damage to your income, which could potentially extend for a long period of time. Being jobless is one thing that could lead to many things, like starvation or homelessness. Aside from losing your job, injury or illness may lead to the same dismal ending—no income for months. This type of burden is equally as devastating as being a victim of a hurricane or other natural disaster.

All of these are major problems. Having enough funds to provide food for your family is the only security that can shrug the stress off your shoulders. You can add other essentials like medicine, utility bills and housing costs as necessary for your family's security and safety.

A three month stock of supplies is a good start. From there, extending your resources to cover a year would surely give you the assurance that, whatever happens along the way, your family is secure for the entire year.

Shelter and Security

The 72-hour kit is a tent for temporary refuge. It includes equipment that can aid you in weathering a disaster, even in the cases of high risk emergencies that are chemical or biological. Also, safety is essential, especially for long-term emergencies. That is why the following should be put into serious consideration for inclusion in your 72-hour kit:

- Sanitary equipment and hygienic kits.
- Heaters and fuel for food preparation.
- Self-defense kits and materials.
- Gadgets for communication and recreation.

* * *

Building the foundation in these four areas is the best way for you to ensure that you and your family are safe and secure. These aspects will equip you with not only enough resources, but also the skills to survive even the most incapacitating periods of your life.

Are you overwhelmed at the thought of creating a survival prep kit?

Perhaps one of the most substantial hurdles an individual must overcome when it comes to establishing and following through with a survival prep kit is the feeling of being overwhelmed. Creating an effective survival plan is a complex and dynamic process. With so many elements to consider, where do you even start?

While you may understand the importance of creating a survival plan, it's far too easy to put these thoughts on the back-burner to be reviewed at a later time. Although it's easy to put things off until tomorrow, what if tomorrow an emergency situation happens? That's the thing about emergencies; you never know when they'll occur. Even though the elements involved in establishing a survival plan can be complex, with this guide you'll find the necessary steps to create and implement an effective survival plan without the stress.

It's essential that you understand that even the smallest steps toward the implementation of a survival plan are important, and soon, after you've made this a priority in your life, you'll have a full-fledged plan and kit.

Although you may have a desire to create a survival plan, you may feel trapped because you don't have expendable income. The desire to create a survival plan is real for many people, but like you the financial ability to do so is limited. It is important to remember not to give up. You aren't required to buy everything needed at one time.

Within this guide, you'll find the necessary steps to create a fully functioning survival plan that doesn't require a second mortgage to accomplish. In fact, almost anyone on any budget can prepare for the future safety of their family without going broke. The following is an overview of what this book covers:

- How to create an effective 72-hour emergency kit capable of sustaining you and your family for three days.
- Storage suggestions for long-term survival. This portion is broken down into two primary parts: three-month supply and 12-month supply guides.
- How to safely and securely establish shelter for you and your family. Within this portion you'll uncover suggestions for a three-month shelter and a 12-month shelter.
- Monthly goals and skills to undertake. This guide breaks down a single goal you should accomplish each month, which leads to a more prepared survival kit.

Within each of the aforementioned sections, you'll receive a step-by-step guide on what you should do every month to reach the final goal of being fully prepared. At the conclusion of 12 months, you'll not only have expanded your knowledge regarding survival techniques, but will also have an effective survival kit capable of sustaining you and your family. While this guide is written to be accomplished in 12 months, it can be altered to fit any time duration and budget.

That being noted, if you plan on following this guide so it is completed within the allotted 12-month time span, be prepared to invest a decent amount of money each month for supplies. Even though the guide offers numerous money-saving tips and techniques, it's impossible to become fully prepared without some financial investment.

Unfortunately, not every reader can afford to follow these guidelines to the letter. If you're finding the financial investment requirements are too expensive, the guide can be adapted to fit your budget. For example, within a single month you may not be able to afford the necessary supplies for the 72-hour emergency kit as well as items for long-term storage. If this is the case, simply focus on gathering items for the 72-hour emergency kit during that month, and then move on to items for long-term storage the following month.

As a general rule of thumb, the 72-hour emergency kit should be the first goal you meet. This kit contains essential items you'll need for a short-term emergency, which could happen at any time. If this is your primary goal, then you may take longer than a month to gather all other supplies. The most important element to remember while following this guide is to move forward. While your pace may be slower than suggested by the guide, some action is better than no action.

Another suggestion for those seeking to become better prepared on a budget is to focus on one element of the guide for numerous years. For example, you're unable to afford to follow all of the suggestions. Therefore, you spend the next four years gathering supplies and food for the three-month survival kit. At the conclusion of this four-year time period, you'll have enough food to feed your family for one complete year.

Of course, the most effective action plan is to follow the guides in this book to the letter. If you're able to do so, you'll be completely prepared for any type of emergency or natural disaster within one calendar year. While you may have this desire, you must also be realistic with your abilities. Remember, this isn't a "go big or go home" scenario. Rather, you should do the best you can with what resources you currently have a. The premise of this entire plan is to simply improve your preparedness. Even if you're only able to do one small kit, this is more than what you previously had.

Throughout each chapter, you'll notice your goals toward becoming more self-reliant increase. The desire to live a prepared lifestyle is one that grows with time and ability. As time progresses, you'll likely find yourself seeking out new skills, discovering new ways to save money and improving your overall health so you'll be strong and reliable in case of a disaster.

* * *

Even if you're unable to complete the guides within the suggested one-year time frame, set an attainable monthly goal. This will not only enrich your life, but it begins the progression of becoming more self-reliant and confident in your ability to care for yourself, your family and your community in case of a natural disaster or emergency.

Stop Thinking and Start Doing – Getting Started

So what if it takes you three years to gather all the necessary supplies and equipment to become truly prepared? The truth of the matter, even the smallest survival kits set you apart from the majority of the population who hang on to their delicate lives with a nothing more than a string.

When you have the knowledge and supplies this book provides, you'll know you can survive in an emergency situation. You won't have to live in fear, and more importantly, you won't be living in blissful ignorance like the bulk of society. These small steps work toward a long-term goal of peace.

One Thing to Remember

Perhaps one of the most important elements to remember in regards to food storage is to only store foods you actually enjoy. Sure, in a genuine emergency or disaster you'll be happy to have any food, but in truly stressful and dire situation the foods you enjoy do far more than fuel your body. Comfort foods do just that, they comfort. When society crumbles, whether due to an economic collapse or a natural disaster, you're not going to be thinking about calories or fat grams. Rather, you're going to be longing for a taste of the familiar. Therefore, treat yourself and your family by storing foods everyone enjoys along with essential foods for survival.

Remember, when selecting foods, choose ones that you and your family enjoy. You'll be surprised how such a small element can mean the difference between optimism and distress.

Month One

"Great things are not done by impulse, but by a series of small things brought together."
-Vincent Van Gogh

The focus this month will be to lay a solid foundation for effective preparation and survival. You will start with a few tasks that are fairly simple and easy to complete. And when combined with several other tasks over the next few months, you will find that they are extremely valuable.

To start, you should schedule a family meeting to discuss all the goals and targets you have for the entire year. You should also clarify the reasons for making such detailed preparations. However, if you are not married, you can tell a close friend about the goals you have set and the plans you will be making.

The Three-Day Survival Kit (The 72-Hour Kit)

Your three-day survival kit should be your first defensive strategy. If you are operating on a tight budget, this is your first goal. Even if you can't complete all the other tasks for this month, make sure you do this one. Here are the things to put in your three-day survival kit:

- A little cash savings, $50 dollars would do for a start. But if you can't save up to $50, save as much as possible. Every little bit helps.

- A big box of safety matches (waterproof).
- A hobby or utility knife.
- A plastic bucket (with a 5-gallon capacity).
- A shovel.
- Sufficient clothing for each family member including shoes, socks, gloves and underwear.
- Add warm coats and winter boots if you live in a cold region.
- A knapsack for each family member including children.

When you are selecting clothes, remember to pick long pants and long-sleeved tops. This type of clothing will protect your body if you have to wade through debris. It will also shield you from the effects of cold weather. However, you may need to include an extra layer of clothing if you reside in an extremely cold region.

Carefully arrange the clothes for each person in their respective knapsacks. Put the money in a purse and place it in your knapsack. Then put the knife and shovel in the plastic bucket.

Next, you should choose a suitable place to keep your three-day survival kit. Make sure you store it in a place that will be easy to reach, so you can quickly pick them up and leave your home. The garage or a closet very close to the rear exit of your house may be a good location.

Extended Food Preservation

* * *

Canned foods are the best option for extended food preservation. The food will remain in good condition for a very long time. In the concluding part of this guide, we will provide valuable tips on how to ensure that your canned foods do not expire in storage. During the month, you should collect the following:

- 6 cans of fish, beef or chicken per head for 3 months' supply, or
- 24 cans of fish, beef or chicken per head for 12 months' supply and
- A durable manually operated can opener.

Next, you should have a suitable space to arrange all your food supplies. You could even acquire special shelves for this purpose. Although there's not much to gather this month, your supplies will accumulate quickly. However, if you don't have adequate space at home, do not be disturbed about it. There are several creative ideas you can use to get the space needed to store your food supplies. Simply make sure you store them in a cool dry place and avoid extremely hot or cold temperatures.

Here are some places where you can keep your food supplies:

- Keep them on the overhead shelves or cabinets in your kitchen.
- Place them below end tables and shield them using a table cloth.
- Arrange them in a storage shed with good climate

control.
- Keep them on shelves in your basement.
- Allocate an entire closet for your supplies.
- Place them under your bed in boxes or plastic bins.

If you ever feel that you are investing too much to store these food supplies, you should consider how valuable these items will be when you need them.

Cleanliness and Hygiene

During the first month and the following two, you will need to gather items to maintain personal hygiene and cleanliness.

- For three months, collect 10 large garbage sacks per head (100 per year)
- For three months, collect half a gallon of bleach per head (1 gallon per year)
- For three months, reserve 2 pounds of laundry detergent per head (20 gallons per year)

Bonus Money Saving Tip: Produce your laundry detergent at home. It will weigh less and save you money. Here's a formula to produce homemade detergent. Mix the following:

- Fels-Naptha soap (3 bars) or Zote (2 bars) — the bars should be grated
- Arm and Hammer washing soda (One 55 ounce box)
- Arm and Hammer baking soda (4 pounds)
- Borax (Two 12 ounce boxes)

- OxyClean (3.5 pounds or 2 small containers) — an optional stain remover

This formula will produce 2 gallons of powered detergent which should last nearly 6 months for an average home. You can produce two batches for the entire year and store them in a 5 gallon container.

Monthly Preparation Goal

Full Domestic Fire Preparation and Protection

Throughout the month, develop a plan to successfully escape from your house if there is a fire outbreak. Create a fire drill every week to put your plan into practice. This will make it easy for everyone to do the right thing if there's an actual fire incident.

An escape plan requires multiple strategies. Therefore, you should practice using various exits just in case any one of them gets blocked. In addition, you should preserve all vital documents in a fireproof cabinet. Fireproof cabinets are not expensive. The documents you should preserve include: automobile titles, home title deeds, insurance papers and the credentials of all family members.

This month, you should also replace the batteries in your smoke detector if they are more than six months old. It is very important to make adequate plans to handle a domestic fire emergency.

* * *

Keep Accurate Records

You need to keep accurate inventory of the items and supplies you have gathered. As your supplies increase, you could easily lose count of what you have obtained and what you still need to add. Besides, keeping accurate inventory helps you to rotate and remove items that are about to expire and replace them with new ones.

A legal pad with ruled sheets and a pen can be used to keep inventory. You could also use a spreadsheet application on your computer or tablet. As soon as you collect your items, you should record the date, the items gathered, their quantity and expiration dates (for food supplies).

Month Two

With a new month comes more information to keep your progress up to speed. If you haven't found a suitable place to safely store away the supplies you have so far, you need to find one soon. The list of items will increase this month so you don't want to scramble around looking for a place to keep them.

What about your inventory sheet? Be sure to keep it up to date with each new supply that you add to your list.

The 72-Hour Kit

The next thing to add to your 72-hour kit is water. Now remember, storing water in plastic gallon containers should be avoided because they have the tendency to break or crack. Your water should be with you at all times, so it's more convenient to carry small bottles of water that will fit in your backpack.

Next, you'll need to gather and make copies of some important personal documents and add additional cash to your emergency kit. Here are the items you'll be adding this month:

- $40 (or more if you can manage)
- One gallon of water (per person)
- Important personal documents (photocopies)

These important documents will include your will, insurance papers, birth certificate, home deed, mortgage papers, passport, automobile titles and a few important business contacts.

To keep these copies safe, store them in a zip-lock plastic bag. This will ensure that no damage is done to the documents regardless of the weather conditions. It's also a good idea to keep the copies on a flash drive for backup, as well as easy accessibility.

However during any emergency, electricity could very well be the first thing you lose, so take good care of those hard copies. The flash drive will only come in handy if the power is restored sooner rather than later.

Gather all of the said items above and pack them in your backpack. The majority of family members shouldn't have a problem with carrying one gallon of water; however, the documents should be kept in one of the adults' backpacks to ensure that they are not misplaced.

Storing Food for Long-Term Purposes

For your food storage this month, we're adding pasta and flour to the list. Here's what you'll need per person:

- 3-month supply – 25 pounds of flour/pasta
- 1-year supply – 100 pounds of flour/pasta

Now, one method of storage is by buying refined flour and storing it in an airtight container. Keep in mind, flour does have an expiration date, which is usually about a year after the date of manufacture. It is also important to note that the flour can also get weevils if not stored properly.

* * *

Placing a few bay leaves on top of the flour is a good way to prolong its life. The leaves help to keep vermin away. You could also consider purchasing whole grains (wheat).

If you didn't already know, wheat can be stored and used for up to three decades or longer. So on the one hand, it saves you the trouble of replacing your stored flour every year; however on the other hand, whole grain cannot be used until you grind it into flour. The choice is yours.

Opting to store whole grains will mean you'll also require a hand mill. While wheat can easily be ground in an electric mill, certain emergencies may leave you with a power outage as we mentioned earlier; therefore, it's important to have a hand mill or your wheat will be of no use.

If you've never milled flour before, we suggest you learn how to so that you are well prepared. When disaster strikes, there are many things you'll find yourself stressing about. Don't let how to make flour be one of them.

* * *

As far as dried pasta is concerned, a sealed package will not go bad for several years. To prolong its life store the sealed package in an airtight container.

Shelter and Security

Now it's time to discuss the sewing kit that you will need to store for long-term purposes. This kit will require these items: needles, thread, a pair of scissors, buttons, zippers, straight pins and velcro.

Including spare fabric in the kit could prove useful for patchwork in case of any tears or damage to your clothes.

The sewing kit can be stored in a metal box container or a zip lock plastic bag and kept along with your food storage.

Money Saving Tip: You can use any of the items in your 72-hour kit for long-term needs as well. For instance, the big bucket that you got last month may be used for long-term sanitation purposes.

By simply putting a garbage bag inside the bucket, it can become a makeshift toilet. After using it, take out the garbage bag, dispose it and line the bucket with a new one. By now, you should have collected all the items on the list for last month, so you will have everything you need to make this temporary sanitation system.

Monthly Preparation Goal

Let's put your skills to the test this month. Have you tried your hand at gardening? If not, take some time off to learn how to sprout seeds. You'll need fresh produce along with your food storage for long-term needs.

In a matter of weeks you can have fresh vegetables by sprouting seeds. Even better, you could grow your own produce in a garden for family meals. Although not everyone has a green thumb, reading a 'how to garden' book or taking a few gardening classes is enough to learn the skills required to grow your own fresh produce.

For those who live in apartment buildings, not to worry; you may carry on with your gardening endeavors by using plant pots or containers. You should keep the plants on your windowsill or patio in order for them to get some sunlight. Not only will you save money by growing your own garden, but you also get the treat of fresh vegetables.

Don't wait for an emergency to begin gardening; start now so that you can improve your gardening skills for when you really need it. Once you expand your garden and the produce quantity increases, you can begin storing the vegetables, which in turn, becomes a savings.

Month Three

"Determination and perseverance move the world; thinking that others will do it for you is a sure way to fail."
-*Marva Collins*

There are times when starting a project is simple and easy; however, after a few months, the motivation that once drove your desires begin to wane. The key to success is not desire, but rather perseverance. This is especially true when it comes to being self-reliant in terms of emergency preparation.

Perhaps one of the most important elements to remember when it comes to preparing your home and family is that you don't have to worry about getting it all done at one time. This being said, if you stop your forward momentum now, it'll be nearly impossible to reach the end goal of being truly prepared.

Throughout this month, recommit yourself to your original goal of self-reliance. Even if life is determined to not give you ample free time, remain steadfast in your quest. The size and scope of your goals shouldn't determine your desire and motivation, even if you're only gathering supplies for your 72-hour emergency preparedness kit.

72 Hour Emergency Kit

This month, even today, it's time to start reviewing the items in your 72 hour emergency kit. The first step is to ensure this kit has ample food for you and your entire family.

Food items found in this kit are those that don't require heat in order to be edible. The ideal foods are those that can be simply opened and consumed. The following list contains food items all emergency kits should contain; however, if you find one or all of these items to be less than desirable, substitute for a similar item.

The most important element to remember is to make sure all food items carry as many calories as possible. This is essential when food rations are short, and stomachs are hungry.

During this initial month, collect the following food items:

- 1 pound of dried fruit or trail mix per person – you can also use fruit leather

- 1 pound package of saltines per person

- 1 box graham crackers per person

- 2 liters of juice per person – tomato and orange are recommended but you can use any juice you like

- $40

The juice you choose must be shelf-stable. That is, the juice doesn't require refrigeration in order to remain fresh and drinkable. Remember, you must replace each juice container once every six months to maintain its safety. While some may not understand the value of juices, they provide ample sugars and nutrients, which are vital during an emergency situation.

After you've collected the aforementioned items, safely secure them in an emergency backpack. Each member of your household must have their own backpack as every person is responsible for carrying and looking after their own food supply. Why? In the horrific event someone in your household was to be separated from your group, they'll have the supplies needed to remain healthy for at least 72 hours.

Long-Term Food Storage

During this month, your focus is not only on creating a 72 hour emergency backpack, but also adding canned food items to your long-term food storage kit. Along with canned foods, you'll be gathering various household items you use regularly as well as starting your long-term water supply.

During this month, focus on gathering the following items:

- 15 cans of soup per person for a 3 month supply, 50 cans for a year supply

- 1 pound of salt per person for a 3 month supply, 5 pounds for a year supply

- 2 pounds of fat per person for a 3 month supply, 20 pounds for a year supply

- 5 gallons of water per person for a 3 month supply, 20 gallons of water for a year supply

- 2 rolls aluminum foil and plastic wrap, 100 gallon size resealable bags for a 3 month supply, 8 rolls aluminum foil and plastic wrap and 400 gallon size bags for a year supply

To prevent confusion, the fats that should be gathered are oils or shortening. Most survival experts suggests 50% of fats come from oils and 50% of fats come from shortening. While some may wish to store butter, without proper cool storage containers, long-term butter storage is quite difficult. If you choose to store butter, you must freeze it to keep it safe.

Consider keeping water in food safe barrels, and when storing 100 gallons or more of water, keep the containers outside, just in case they leak .

$ Saving Tip. Money-Saving Tip: Repurpose 2-liter soda bottles by storing water in them. If you don't drink soda, ask your friends or other family members to donate their used soda bottles. By filling these bottles with tap water, you'll save an exponential amount of money since you won't have to purchase pre-filled water bottles. If you go this route, make sure to clean and sanitize the interior soda bottles with soapy water, followed by a thorough rinse. Once you've refilled the bottles, write that days date on the bottle with permanent marker.

To make sure you have no microbes growing in the bottles, soak them in a sink filled with water and one cup of bleach.

Make sure the bottles get filled as much as possible and turn them over so that all surfaces touch the water. 10 minutes should sanitize them well. Don't forget to add the lids.

Sterilizing Soda Bottles for Water Storage

While 2-liter bottles are a cost-effective way of meeting water rations, it's essential to sterilize these bottles, especially if they've been sitting empty for some time. To sterilize, place one cup of bleach into a sink full of water.

Submerge the bottles and allow them to fully soak for 10 minutes. Drain the bleach water out of the bottles and allow them to sit, without their lids, for 24-hours. Make sure the interior of the bottles are completely dry before filling with water. If you're using chlorinated water, simply fill the bottles, screw on their lid and place in a dark room.

If the water you're using is not chlorinated, you're going to have to add bleach into the water. While it may seem odd, bleach will prevent bacteria growth. As a general rule of thumb, for every gallon of water, add 8 drops of bleach. Therefore, for a 2-liter soda bottle, you'll only need four drops of bleach to prevent the water from growing harmful bacteria. Use only pure bleach; not bleach with additives or fragrances.

Keep all water stored in a cool, dry environment free from direct sunlight. Keep the bottles on shelving; not on your basement floor.

* * *

Shelter and Security

Along with gathering supplies for your short and long-term preparedness kits, this month begin inspecting your home for safety issues. It's vital that homeowners investigate and fix various safety issues before a disaster strikes. Doing so allows you to focus on your family during the crisis, and not your home.

When inspecting the inside of your home, make sure you carefully check electrical cords for fraying which could lead to a fire. This is especially important if you have pets or children, as electrical cords could be damaged due to chewing or improper handling. Make sure to check electrical cords found under furniture.

Ensure all electrical and digital devices are plugged into a surge protector; not directly into the wall. Consider purchasing battery backup units, if you don't already have them, and make sure all carbon monoxide and fire alarms are in working order. If you don't have one, purchase a minimum of one fire extinguisher.

Review the plumbing of your home for leaks and other issues. Walk throughout your home and open and close all windows to make sure they're operable. If a window is unable to be easily opened, closed, and locked, take care of this ASAP.

An additional purchase that may be essential is an escape ladder. This is essential if your home is multiple stories. In the unfortunate event of a home fire, home invasion or some other natural disaster, escape ladders may mean the difference between life or death.

While you should have an escape route for your house, it's essential to regularly walk through this route to ensure it's not blocked. Make sure clutter and furniture are free from these routes.

Moving on to the exterior of your home, secure all items on your patio or porch that could fly away. This includes grills, toys and furniture. If you live in an area that's prone to natural disasters, such as tornadoes or hurricanes, this step is crucial. Make sure all flammable items are stored away from your home. Review the quality of all fuel lines, and upgrade or replace as necessary.

Regularly remove debris from your gutters so rainwater can easily flow, which prevents leaks from infiltrating your home. While reviewing your gutters, scan over your roofing shingles and replace them as needed.

While you inspected the interior of your windows and doors, now's the time to inspect them from the outside. Consider sealing all windows and doors with weather-resistant paint. Make sure all pipes in and outside of your home are insulated. This is essential if you live in a climate that sees freezing temperatures during winter months.

Lastly, make sure your house numbers are clearly visible on the exterior of your home. If possible, paint your house number on the curb in front of your home. This is important in case the house numbers are damaged during a disaster, or removed during a home invasion.

Monthly Preparation Goal

During this month, make it a priority to ensure all of your vehicles always have a minimum of a half tank of gas at all times. When you see fuel levels starting to approach the half-tank mark, go ahead and refuel.

This step is essential to make sure you always have ample gas to escape an area during an emergency evacuation. When a natural disaster strikes, gasoline is the first element to become scarce. Prevent being stranded by ensuring all cars are filled with gas at all times.

Month Four

"Failing to prepare is like preparing to fail."
-John R. Wooden

At this point, you should be a quarter of the way through with your survival preparations for the year. Just take a moment to sit back and think about all of your hard earned accomplishments! This month you will be adding a whole lot more food to your Long-term Food Storage and 72-Hour Kits. You will also be taking various security options into consideration.

The 72-Hour Kit

There is a little more food that you will need to add to the 72-Hour Kit this month, and best of all this food is also easy to prepare and eat. It does not require any special attention or handling. The list for this month is light, because you will be adding way more food to the Long-Term Storage Kit.

This month you will need for each person:

- 4 granola bars.
- 2 sticks of beef jerky.
- 1 package of chewing gum.
- At least 12 hard candies or lollipops.
- $40 cash (or as much as you can put back).

Candy may not seem like a necessary supply for the kit, but

sugar is known to give quick calories and can even provide a sense of comfort, especially during difficult times of emergency.

Long-Term Food Storage

For this month your primary focus will be on food supplies. Each person in your family will need:

- A 1/2 pound of yeast to last for 3 months, or 2 pounds for a year.
- A 1/2 pound of baking powder to last for 3 months, or 2 pounds for a year.
- A 1/4 pound of baking soda to last 3 months. 1 pound per person will last an entire year.
- 1 quart of vinegar to last for 3 months, or 1 gallon for one year.
- 3 cans of evaporated milk to last for 3 months, or 10 cans for a year.
- 5 pounds of peanut butter (or any butter made from nuts) to last for 3 months, or 20 pounds for a year.
- Spices, various condiments, vanilla, etc.

You most likely will notice that you are only storing food ingredients as opposed to real food. This is because processed foods do not last for long on a shelf and will go bad over time. Take a loaf of bread for instance. It will go bad and become moldy after a mere few weeks of sitting on the counter.

However, with these important and necessary items, you

will be able to bake your own bread every day and you won't have to worry about expiration dates. When dealing with long-term survival, the typical family will bake a loaf of bread every day.

For condiments, it is best to stock up on things that you and your family enjoy, such as mayonnaise, ketchup, mustard, etc. When dealing with spices, stock up on cinnamon, paprika, Italian seasoning, etc.

An excellent tip for saving money is to buy your cooking and baking items in bulk at the food warehouse. If you simply go ahead and get the year's supply of the items, it will save you a lot more money in the long run.

Shelter and Security

This month you will need to consider defense strategies and security for your family, especially during emergency situations or potential safety risks. Some people prefer to stock up on firearms for defense, while others might not agree with this method.

In times of long-term emergencies, and especially when electricity and power are down, you will need to be constantly aware of looters and other highly dangerous people who will use violence to get what they want in order to survive.

It is actually extremely necessary to have weapons and ammunition available during these troublesome circumstances; furthermore it is especially important to have proper training with safe handling and use. At least stock up on pepper spray, or anything that will help defend you and your family from danger.

If you think firearms are a great choice, take the time this month to look for a proper course on safe use and defense strategies. You should also start putting some money back in order to purchase dependable firearms and ammunition, and teach family lessons on safety and proper firearm storage.

Monthly Preparation Goal

During the month, it is highly beneficial and recommended that you learn how to make your own bread from scratch. You should have all the proper ingredients now in the Long-Term Storage Kit. The following is an excellent recipe for baking your own bread, and all you need is an oven.

- 4 1/2 cups of whole wheat flour.
- 1 1/2 cups of lukewarm water.
- A 1/4 cup of honey.
- 2 tablespoons of olive or vegetable oil.
- 1 teaspoon of salt.
- 2 1/4 teaspoons of yeast.

Start the recipe by proofing the yeast. Next, mix the honey and water in a large bowl, then sprinkle the yeast on top. Let this sit for about 10 minutes. The yeast will begin to look frothy when it is ready to go.

Next, add the oil and salt to the mix, and then add one cup of whole wheat flour at a time, while mixing. You need to mix the dough until it is no longer sticky, and then lay it out on a floured surface to knead for about 10 minutes.

Place the bread in a bowl covered in plastic wrap or a damp towel, and wait about an hour for it to rise, or until it is doubled. Then, press the dough back down to its original size, and form it into a nice bread loaf. Next, just place the loaf in a bread loaf pan.

Preheat your oven to 350 degrees Fahrenheit and allow the loaf to rise for approximately 30 minutes, until it is again doubled in size. Then just place it in the oven for 25-30 minutes. When the time is up, let the bread cool off for 10 minutes, and then remove it from the bread loaf pan to finish cooling.

Although it can be time consuming, bread is really easy to make, and homemade bread is actually really tasty. As soon as you master this skill, you will be more prepared if an emergency occurs preventing you from buying a loaf at the supermarket.

The recipe provided is a really simple method to making bread from scratch, however there are many other options available to make the bread you and your family love. Whole grain breads are much healthier choices for nutrition.

Month Five

Freedom comes from strength and self-reliance.
-Lisa Murkowski

This month's selection of survival preparation items will include supplies that are essential for your 72-hour kit. These items may also be used as part of your long-term survival needs. Since a majority of the items included in this month's kit will require you to invest in several items, there will not be a cash addition to this month's supplies.

However, if you are able to set aside at least $40 extra for your emergency funds, it will make things go much smoother for you over time and help you reach your goal of saving around $500 by the end of the year. This money needs to be saved in cash and not in a checking or savings account in case there are issues with power systems, computers or other forms of communication.

While $500 is not enough to live on when it comes to survival, it will be enough to help you purchase shelter or food if needed. You can use the cash to cover the cost of a few nights in a motel, which will provide you with some time to come up with a more permanent living space.

The 72-Hour Kit

At this point, you should already have enough food stored away for three day's survival. This kit is designed to take care of your other essential needs that will make survival bearable. You may already have several of these items at home, but if you do not it is time to gather them up and store them with your other emergency items.

These Items Include:

- $40 Emergency Cash
- Kerosene Lamps
- Kerosene
- Battery Operated Radio
- Batteries
- Battery Powered Light such as a Flashlight or Camping Lantern

You can find multipurpose tools that can help save you time, money and space in your emergency kit. Look for a radio that serves as a weather or news radio, and one that includes an electronics charger or lantern. While these items may cost extra, they will prove to be very beneficial in the long run. You can also find lights or radios that do not require batteries, such as solar charged lights or weather radios that can be hand-cranked in order to operate for several hours. It is a good idea to look for items like these that will allow you to save your batteries for other emergency uses.

Long-Term Food Storage

This month you will need to add a large amount of grains to your food storage. You will also want to add sweets that will provide you with an energy boost while on the go, and seeds to use for gardening. Gather the following items for each person in your group.

- 25 lbs. of grains such as cornmeal, oatmeal, barley or rice. This will be enough grains for three months' time. Gather up 100 lbs. for an entire year.
- Packages of flavored gelatin (6 packs for 3 months, 24 packs for a year).
- Garden seeds – Choose a variety that you and your group will enjoy.
- Seeds for Sprouting

When you are buying grains, choose varieties that you and the other members of your group already enjoy eating. If you do not prefer gelatin, you can go with another type of non-perishable dessert such as brownie mix or chocolate chips. These will be considered comfort foods and are essential for survival preparation and boost morale.

Shelter & Security

Items to add for shelter and security this month will include various hygiene supplies that you will not want to live without, such as:

- Rolls of toilet paper for each person in your group (24 rolls for a 3 month supply, 100 rolls per person for a year).
- 80-count packs of baby wipes (3 per person for 3 months, 12 per person for a year's supply, more if there are children still in diapers at the time).

* * *

These two items are extremely beneficial for keeping up personal hygiene. Baby wipes can be used for bathing if water is not always available.

Monthly Preparation Goal

It is important that you learn to be as self-reliant as possible, and in order to do so you must add items to your emergency kit that will help you grow a garden. You will also need items that will help you preserve food by drying fruit and meat, or canning vegetables. If you are unable to grow your own garden due to limited space, you can look for produce sales at your local supermarket.

If you have the extra space but lack the green thumb and general knowledge for growing a garden, you can pick up books or sign up for a local class in your community that will teach you gardening skills. There are also many tutorials available online that can help you produce a variety of fruits and vegetables that will help keep you and your family fed.

Month Six

"The greatest risk in life is to wait for and depend upon others for your own security."
-Denis Waitley

Being ready for emergencies and having a well laid out future plan to meet your needs is one of the requirements in today's life. By the end of this month, we would like you to be almost done with emergency preparedness. This month we are going to lay our focus on first aid and the use of first aid kit items. This kit is going to be part of your 72-hour emergency kit and your long-term storage kit.

The chapter below mainly focuses on first aid since it encompasses all of the other sections.

The First Aid Kit

The following materials constitute the minimum requirements every aid kit should have. However, depending on the needs of your family, additional items might need to be included. For instance, if you have a baby in your family, certain medications prescribed for children might be required.

Basic First Aid Requirements

This list includes:

- Antibiotic ointment.

- Calamine lotion.
- First aid instruction book.
- Breathing barrier for CPR.
- 25 adhesive bandages of different sizes.
- An adhesive tape which measures about 10 yards.
- Aspirin.
- Ibuprofen.
- A pair of scissors.

In addition to the above items, the list should also have:

- A thermometer.
- Soap.
- Two triangular bandages.
- Two elastic wraps.
- Hydrogen peroxide.
- Razor blades.
- Tweezers.
- At least one emergency blanket.
- Ten gauze bandages.
- Hydrocortisone ointment.
- Diarrhea remedy medication.
- Safety pins.
- Instant cold compress.
- Measuring cup.
- Two pairs of non-latex gloves.
- A wound cleaning agent like sealed moistened towelettes.

When it comes to materials like general medications, ointments and alcohol, it is recommended to put them in small sized packets to leave space for other items in the kit. But for convenience purposes in the long term, you might use full size packets. If you also nurse certain ailments, you may need to have a consistent supply of prescription drugs alongside other medications. Even though it's recommended to have a large variety of prescription drugs, a one-month supply is enough due to restrictions.

The kit sometimes does not have everything that you need. This means that you might have to add them to your list and maybe put them in another container. Usually, special equipment such as tubing, syringes and bed pads may need to be sourced from somewhere else and put in a different container if the kit is full. Sharp objects such as needles and razors are supposed to be kept in a hard plastic container or a heavy vinyl bag. However, as a caution, disposable plastic bags should never be used.

Money Saving Tip: In order to save more money, it's advisable to buy a pre-made first aid kit since it has most of the items and this makes it easy to add other items that you will need. Buying a brand new first aid kit has its own advantages. One of them is that you will get a carrying case for the kit and the second is that you will save more compared to buying each individual item.

Money for Emergency: Adding only $40 to your emergency kit every month will make you have higher savings in the long-term.

Monthly Preparation Goal

* * *

Since the kit is at your disposal for now, you should know how to use the items it contains. In case you don't know how to use the items, it's high-time to train with a first aid expert. One of the best first aid training grounds is the Red Cross. The cost of the training course is usually affordable and takes a short time.

Month Seven

"There's no harm in hoping for the best as long as you're prepared for the worst."
— *Stephen King*

Congratulations to you for working over half a year in order to take care of your family; hopefully you've accomplished enough these past few months to provide more safety and security. You are most likely doing much better now than before you began; regardless of whether or not you have gone through every step or just focused on one specific area.

However, you are not finished just yet! During this month you will be stocking up more items in your food storage, taking extreme consideration for infant and young child needs, and adding even more supplies to your 72-hour kit.

The 72-Hour Kit

This month you need to focus on emergency shelter necessities. If you do not already have these items , make it a goal to purchase them or start putting money aside for them. However, if you already have them keep them grouped together somewhere safe with your other emergency kit supplies.

- A few tents depending on the size of your family.
- Enough sleeping bags for everyone.
- Emergency blankets for each person (Mylar Space Blankets are recommended).

- Entertainment items to help with boredom, or anything   to help occupy your time (there is going to be a lot of free time)!
- A reliable camp stove with the right type of fuel (Some newer camp stoves even have ovens built in).
- Mosquito repellent.
- $40 cash as an emergency fund.

If you already have some of these items, it is highly important to make sure they are reliable and sufficient for survival. You should inspect equipment every 6 months, especially if it has not been used in a while.

Long-Term Food Storage

This month you will be adding some basic cooking and baking supplies to food storage. The list here is a little shorter due to the demanding list of 72-Hour Kit supplies. Each person in the family will need these highly important items.

- At least 4 pounds of sugar to last for 3 months. That is about 50 pounds in one year.
- 1 #10 can of powdered milk is enough to last for 3 months. 10 #10 powdered milk cans will last a year.
- Baby formula, if you have an infant or small child.
- Baby food, if applicable.

Powdered milk can be used for both baking and drinking. However, the taste of powdered milk is not desirable, so you can add a teaspoon of vanilla for every quart of milk made in order to improve the flavor. If you are lucky enough to have an electrical supply, it is best to mix the milk with vanilla and then refrigerate overnight to get the best taste.

Shelter and Security

This month you will also need to add more to your list of hygiene supplies, as well as proper supplies for an infant. Add enough of these items to your storage supplies in order to last one full year for each person in your family.

- At least 3 toothbrushes.
- 6 tubes of toothpaste.
- 1 large bottle of mouthwash.
- Diapers (it is much easier and economical to use cloth diapers as opposed to disposables).
- A baby food grinder.
- Baby lotion, powder, and anything to keep your baby clean with good hygiene.

The reason there is no definite amount to the list of baby needs is because this depends on the size and age of the child. Make the best decision you see fit to keep your child clean and properly nourished for a year.

Monthly Preparation Goal

If you have not been camping lately, then this is the best month to do so, and you can get more experienced and prepared for survival! Get some good practice in on using your camp stove, tent and other survival items. Depending on the climate conditions, you may have to plan a camping trip, but just do it while the weather is still nice! It is an excellent and fun way to enjoy nature and the outdoors, as well as putting your survival skills to the test. You do not want an emergency evacuation to be the first time you put your tent together. That is why it is always best to already know what you are doing, and always have a game plan for when the situation arises.

Month Eight

"Be prepared!"
-Boy Scout Motto

During this month, your primary focus will be adding more food to your long-term storage kit as well as to your 72-hour emergency kit. Along with increasing the number of food items, if you have pets you'll begin outlining and preparing for their needs. Although many consider their pets members of their family, the majority of survival preppers forget to include them in their survival plans.

Increasing Your 72-Hour Emergency Kit Food Storage

Throughout this month, you'll focus on adding proteins and eating utensils to the kit. Along with the aforementioned, you'll also begin adding items for any and all pets.

Focus on collecting the following items:

- One can of tuna for each person in your household.
- One can of pork and beans for each person in your household.
- Half-Pound of dried milk for each person in your household.
- Two packets of instant hot chocolate mix for each person in your household.
- Two packets of instant soup for each person in your household.
- Disposable bowls, utensils, plates and cups for each

person in your household.
- Additional water for your pet. The exact amount is based upon the type of pet you own.
- Three days' worth of canned or dry pet food for each pet.
- Disposable pet bowls for water and food.
- Sturdy leash for each pet.
- If necessary, a travel crate to keep pets safe during an emergency.
- Bedding for each pet (optional).
- Additional medications for each pet (if required).
- An additional $40 cash storage. Smaller bills are better than larger denominations.

In terms of caring for your pets during a disaster or emergency scenario, it's best to seek out collapsible bowls and other items. Since these items will go into your emergency backpack, it's essential to purchase space-saving items when possible.

Increasing Your Long-Term Food Storage

When you're not adding to your emergency kit, this month requires you to add further nutritional and delicious treats to your long-term food storage kit. Much like the 72-hour kit, you'll be adding items for your pets.

Narrow your focus, and collect the following:

- 3 Month Storage – 25 quarts of vegetables and/or fruits per person.

- 12 Month Storage – 100 quarts of vegetables and/or fruits per person.
- 3 Month Storage – 6 pints of jelly or jam per person.
- 12 Month Storage – 24 pints of jelly or jam per person.
- Dry or Canned Pet Food – exact amounts vary based on pet breed and size.
- Essential Pet Treatments – gather medications such as heartworm or flea treatments.
- Treats for Pets – exact amount and type varies based on pet breed and size.

Should you be required to provide your own food supply for a long period of time, canned vegetables and fruits are the safest way to obtain necessary nutrients outside of growing a garden. To make your money go further, purchase canned vegetables and fruits during the holiday months. This is when the majority of grocery stores have sales on these items.

Enhancing Your Shelter and Security

If your household has any female members, this is the month where you'll begin increasing the number of female-specific items. Before starting, calculate the number of items each female household member uses on a monthly basis. To create a well-rounded long-term kit, multiply the monthly supply by the number of months you're gathering.

Some of the most common items you'll need to gather include:

- Sanitary pads and/or tampons
- Feminine-specific medications, such as yeast infection medications
- Urinary tract infection medications

Once these items have been gathered, shift your focus to accumulating supplies to create an in-place shelter. These items are essential when you must create a secure shelter to prevent radiation or chemicals from infiltrating your safe room. These items may also come in handy if a member of your household contracts a highly contagious illness.

To create a secure and safe shelter gather the following items throughout this month:

- Measure all doors and windows within the room that's designated your "safe room." Once these measurements are taken, purchase 2-4 mm plastic sheeting. These sheets will cover doors, air vents, room openings and all windows within the space.
- One to two rolls of duct tape to secure the plastic sheeting and create an airtight seal.

As a general rule of thumb, choose a room in your home to be your designated safe room before any disaster strikes. This way when your family requires shelter, you already understand where to go, which is essential during chaotic moments. The ideal room is one that's in the interior of your home with as few windows and doors as possible.

Consider a room that's close to where your survival supplies are stored. Perhaps use this room as the official storage space for not only the aforementioned supplies, but also for your 72-hour emergency kits.

Generally, the public is warned through the radio or other public broadcast when a chemical weapon has been deployed. It's during these precious moments that you must gather your family and enter this safe room. Since the spread of chemicals or radiation can happen quickly, keeping these supplies in the room saves time when time truly matters.

While swiftly gathering your family members, make sure you deactivate all air conditioning and heating units. In order to truly secure this room from infiltration by chemicals or radiation, all interior air flow must cease. Establish responsibilities for each family member. For example, one person is responsible for gathering supplies not already in the room, while the other is responsible for turning off the air conditioning or heating unit on their way to the safe room. Consider placing AC unit controls in or near the safe room.

Monthly Preparation Goal

If possible, invest your survival money into a solar oven. This piece of equipment is essential when you run out of electricity or fuel. During a natural disaster, the municipal gas supply systems may be non-operational. Solar ovens work by harnessing the power of the sun and will be able to assist you in continuing to cook meals and sanitize water.

* * *

Much like solar panels provide electricity to power homes, solar ovens convert sun radiation into an electric cooking source. These ovens operate in a strikingly similar manner as traditional ovens. You're able to bake bread, cook casseroles and perfectly tend to meats to ensure they're safe to eat.

The current solar oven marketplace offers a myriad of oven designs and sizes. Choose an oven that's large enough to cook meals for your family, but small enough to be stored away without taking too much room. The weight of an oven should come into consideration, especially if you must evacuate your home, but require a cooking source.

Regardless of the weather, modern solar ovens are able to be powered even during overcast days. Take your time reviewing and testing out a variety of solar ovens to ensure you purchase the ideal product for your specific survival needs.

Month Nine

"For tomorrow belongs to the people who prepare for it today."
-African Proverb

Several items in your 72-hour emergency kit will need to be rotated this month. These are food items that will expire. You should check the expiration dates on these to learn whether or not they need to be replaced. There are several additional food items that will need to be added to your long-term storage as well.

You also have to start thinking about how you are going to stay safe if an outbreak of disease ever occurs in your region.

The 72-Hour Kit

For this month, you just need to rotate a few of the items that are in your kit. If all of your stored food items are still good, this is not a step that you need to worry about. Simply check the expiration dates on each one of these and replace all items that will go bad at any time during the next six months.

The items that have to be checked this month are your trail mix, dried fruit, graham crackers and juice. You want to make sure that these do not go bad so that you have plenty of food during any crisis that makes it necessary for you to leave your home.

* * *

If you are able to do so, put $40 in your emergency kit. At the year's end, you should have at least $500 stored that can be used in the event of an emergency.

Long-Term Food Storage

There are several basic items that you will need to stock up on for long-term food storage. More milk will need to be added to your supplies as will starches and fruit or tomato juice. For each person in the home, you should have the following amounts in supply:

- For one month, three 10 pound cans of powdered milk, for a year's supply, ten 10 pound cans.
- 2 pounds of potatoes either canned or dried for three months or 5 pounds of these for a full year.
- 12 quarts of either tomato or fruit juice for three months or 50 quarts for a full year.

One of the best ways to add starches to your diet through your long-term food storage is by stocking up on instant potatoes. These are easy to get and easy to make. There are also many different flavors that you can choose from if you are not partial to plain potatoes.

You also have the option of using instant potatoes to thicken up your gravies and sauces, make potato cakes or add to breads. The fact that these are so versatile makes them a wonderful addition to your long-term storage.

Security and Shelter

A disease epidemic is something that we have not spent a lot of time talking about but this is a definite possibility. International travel could enable a disease to become a global issue in a very nominal amount of time.

Once every several years or so there is an outbreak of illness, this makes people consider the need to be well prepared. More often than not, however, this is something that people simply push to the backs of their minds until the next major outbreak occurs.

With a good first aid kit and your long-term food storage, you will be able to survive long periods of being home-bound. It is also vital, however, to think about having protection to prevent yourself from becoming ill and to prevent the illness of someone else from affecting your entire group.

You will need to have a number of supplies for preventing the spread of illness that far exceed the contents of your first aid kit, such as:

- A minimum of one Tyvek suit that can be used to guard against contaminants.
- Protective eyewear.
- N95 respirator masks (masks like these are designed to be disposable and thus, you will need to purchase a reasonable number of these based upon this fact).
- A box of non-latex gloves (at least 100).
- Tissues
- Biohazard bags that can be used for the disposal of

biological waste.

You get the best protection from smaller particles with N95 masks as opposed to surgical masks, so spending a bit more to get these is always worthwhile.

You also want to take this time to think about buying a gas mask for every member of the household. These offer a lot more protection than N95 masks because they can protect against both chemical attacks and disease.

Gas masks typically have filters that need to be replaced, so you will want to add a bunch of filters to your store. These, however, can be disinfected and worn again. Due to this fact they could be the most cost-effective option.

When buying gas masks, it is vital to buy one for every person in the home and to ensure that all household members spend time learning how to put these on.

A Tip for Saving $$$ - When preparing for a pandemic you will often find comprehensive kits that contain most of the items on this list. Purchasing one of these kits is a great way to save cash. You will have to make sure to add in any of the items that are on this list and that are not found in your kit.

Monthly Preparation Goal

While you consider the possibility of a disease outbreak, you also want to think of ways that you can bolster and preserve your overall health. If you are healthy before a disaster hits, you will likely fare much better.

Emergencies often require people to walk long distances. These situations can also cause a lot of stress, which in turn diminishes immune system functions. When you are strong, you will have a far better ability to stave off illnesses and to manage the stress of dealing with an emergency event.

To prepare yourself for the unexpected, there are several health goals that you should set. Among these are:

- Take a daily multivitamin.
- Spend five days per week exercising for a minimum of 30 minutes.
- Maintain a diet that is plant based and try to have a daily minimum of 5 servings of vegetables and fruits.
- Drink no less than 64 ounces of water each day.
- Try to get between seven and nine hours of sleep each night.
- Catch health problem before they have a chance to spiral out of control by receiving regular check-ups.

In addition to preserving your well-being during an emergency event, these efforts can also increase your current life quality. Moreover, they will make you more self-reliant and keep you independent. They will additionally help you to reduce your health care costs in the future.

Although it won't be possible to prevent all health issues, many of the chronic illnesses that commonly plague people are directly connected to life choices. It is possible to reduce the risk of chronic fatigue, arthritis, heart disease and diabetes by simply maintaining a lifestyle that is balanced and healthy.

Start working with your loved ones this month to begin establishing a health goal. Try to avoid overdoing it. Simply pick a few steps that can be taken to improve your health and then start working on these.

Month Ten

"If you can meet with Triumph and Disaster,
And treat those two impostors just the same."
-Rudyard Kipling

With the end of the year-long prepper plan coming into sight, it's time to do some rotation work on your 72-hour emergency kit. Other aims to be completed during this month include adding some long-term food supplies, as well as a few basic toiletries.

The 72-Hour Kit

During the previous month you should have rotated food items in the kit and this month you need to do likewise. Check the expiration date on the beef jerky, hard candy and granola bars in your food supplies. If the dates are 6 months or more in the future, these items can be left in place. However, expiration dates that are up in less than 6 months should be rotated and replaced with new items to ensure that your long-term supplies are good for at least 6 months or more. If possible you should also try to add another $40 to the kit by the end of the month.

Long-Term Food Supplies

You should add new items to your long-term food supply this month, and this includes the following for each family member:

- 5 stew, chili, or soup cans to cover a three-month period, 50 of these cans to supply a full year.
- 2 pounds of dried or bottled cheese to cover a 3 month period, 10 pounds to supply a full year.

The type of cheese we are talking about is similar to the powdered variety that can be found in a standard box of dry macaroni and cheese. Find the right kind and it can be stored for a long period of time; this makes it a good choice for survival supplies. Dried cheese is an excellent resource for making sauces and soups, and it can even add some taste to your popcorn. In addition to dried cheese, it is also possible to find shredded cheese for sale these days and this can be just as useful.

Finding a flavor you like should not be a problem, with dried cheddar, mozzarella and many other types available. Simply adding water will re-hydrate it for use in making pizzas, chilies, cheese soup and more. The shelf life of some types can be up to 25 years, meaning that it is a cost effective supply that will be available for use for a long time. A search online will show plenty of options to buy, and it can be sensible to stock your food supplies with a few varieties.

Toiletries and Other Supplies

Food is not the only essential prepper supply required, this month you will add some basic toiletries, cleaning and other supplies. For a start this includes:

- 10 to 12 bottles of dish soap.
- Shaving equipment to suit the number of people that need this.
- Waterproof matches.

While staying in a shelter and using stored food is the best way of surviving, preparation is still needed in case supplies run low. This might mean going outdoors to hunt and fish for additional food, and it is important to have the equipment available for doing this. It is also essential that you know how to use it, so this month is a time to consider buying the equipment needed and obtaining the skills for using it. If family or friends are interested in these outdoor pursuits, ask for their help in learning the basics. Otherwise look to a local outdoor store or other place that provides lessons in hunting and fishing so you can take a class. This should help you understand what to get, as well as the knowledge to effectively use it. Keep in mind, this might just provide the food needed to help you survive.

Preparation Equipment

While matches provide a simple way to start a fire, it is important to know what to do if these are not available. Take some time this month for you and other family members to work on the skill of starting a fire without matches. There are several ways this can be done. Some of these including the following:

- Flint stones and steel.
- A bow drill kit.

- Steel wool along with a battery.
- Harnessing the sun's rays with a lens.

Try to practice each of these ways if possible, so that if matches are not available you are still capable of using other means to get a fire going. This can help to build confidence in your survival abilities. You should also practice finding fuel for a fire. This is most commonly wood. Try to pick out the driest pieces available and a variety of sizes to get a fire started and keep it going. Some practice should get you used to what to look for and make it easier to find what is needed. A fire is obviously important for a number of reasons when outdoors. It is needed for cooking food and can also provide warmth that increases the chances of survival. Also try to understand the correct way to contain a fire when it is burning and how to properly put it out. This type of fire safety is essential to make sure you do not unintentionally set alight anything around a campfire.

Month Eleven

"Success depends upon previous preparation, and without
such preparation there is sure to be failure."
– Confucius

At this point in your preparations you have been at it for a
long time and should have most of the supplies you need
stocked and ready. In the event of the inevitable natural
disaster, outbreak of disease or social breakdown, you
should feel good about your chances of making it through.

You have probably made arrangements for short term
survival needs as well as stockpiled items that will be
needed for the long haul. Let's go over what you should
definitely have available in each of these cases.

The 72-Hour Kit

At this time, you will need to review the items in your 72-
hour kit and make sure that you have made toiletry items
available. If this has not been done, you will want to obtain
the necessary items at once. After doing this it is a good idea
to pre-pack these items in the backpacks you have put aside
for this purpose. The list of items should include the
following:

- Travel size bottles of liquid soap. Liquid is the
  preferred choice because bar soap can dissolve when
  it is saturated. You will want to have at least one
  bottle for everyone in your family.

- Enough toothbrushes and toothpaste for each individual.
- If there is an infant in the family, you should pack diapers, baby formula and infant hygiene products.
- Feminine products.
- Anti-bacterial wipes.
- At least one large roll of aluminum foil.
- A sturdy compass.
- A laminated map of the surrounding areas.
- At least $50 in cash.

Having these personal hygiene items will be of great comfort to the family if and when it becomes necessary for a short-term evacuation. The compass and map are especially important. In the event of an emergency, not only will communications systems be inaccessible, but it is highly likely that electrical power will be unavailable.

Long-Term Preparation

At this stage, you have probably stored many of the items that will be needed in the event of a long term disaster. There are a few items you will want to make available if you haven't already. These items include:

- Wheat. Each person in the family should have at least 10 pounds put aside for 3 months of meals. If you are preparing for a year of survival, put aside 100 pounds per person. Wheat is especially valuable because if it is stored properly it can last for many decades. You may also wish to buy a small container of wheat and get some practice grinding it and preparing it in different ways. Having this skill will be a great advantage when the time comes to apply it.

- 4 to 5 #10 juice mix cans. These survival juices have a shelf life of over 15 years and contain vitamin C. While 4 to 5 cans should last for a year, 1 can should suffice for 3 months of survival.

- Powdered eggs. First, figure out how many eggs each family member will eat per day, and add that number together. Next, take this number and multiply it by 54 weeks. The extra two weeks are to make an allowance for baked goods. Once you have the final number you can purchase the amount needed. Keep in mind that most cans will contain between 12 and 18 dozen eggs.

Shelter and Security

At this point you will have begun making arrangements concerning shelter and security. You will once again want to review your preparations. If not already obtained, you will want to include the following items.

- At least 1 bottle of hand soap each per person. This amount should last about 3 months. To make a one year supply available, each person should have at least 4 bottles.

- Shower gel or body wash. People have different needs in this area, but for a 3 month supply 1 to 2 bottles should be enough. For a one year supply, each individual should have 4 or more.

- Light bulbs. You should carefully store as many light bulbs as are needed to replace every bulb in the home at least once. Modern day low energy fluorescent bulbs are a great choice due to their durability.

Once you have procured and stored these items, it will be time to reassess the true security worthiness of your home. In a functioning society, a good alarm system may be all that is needed. When the electrical grid, food and fuel distribution go down, you will need something a little sturdier.

Home Security

Home security systems do have their place. They will deter certain types of intruders, and at least should alert you to the presence of an unwanted visitor. The problem is all of these systems run on electricity. In order to anticipate a loss of electrical power, whatever system is purchased should have the option of running on solar or battery power. If a battery back-up system is chosen, care should be taken to make sure an adequate number of backup batteries are ready to go at any time.

But this is just the beginning. In some cases, the security system will not work properly. In other cases, you may be up against assailants that don't care if you have one. This is where your second line of defense comes in. This line of defense involves the structural soundness of your home itself.

Let's start with the doors. All of the doors on the exterior of your home should be structurally reinforced with steel plating. This will stop almost any intruder in their tracks. But a door is only as strong as its lock; so to address this possible weakness, doors should have several locks available. These locks should be tamper proofed from the outside to preclude lock picking. Additionally, many modern reinforced doors come with interior barriers that are impossible to access from the outside.

Next let's look at the windows. All of the windows should be able to be locked from the inside of the house. If it is affordable, bulletproof glass can be substituted for the original frames. Barring this, steel shutters can be obtained that can be closed and locked in the event of bad weather or an attempted break in.

Inside the house itself, make sure to put your valuable survival supplies in a secure and locked location. In addition to this, use caution when transferring your supplies into the house. It does not pay to let too many people know that you have a house full of potentially vital survival gear.

An old fashioned but very effective survival security feature is the dog. Having a large and well trained family dog can make a huge difference. They not only will alert you to any outside presence, but they will actively protect you and your family members from danger.

Preparation Drills for the Month

Each month you and your family members should actively do drills that practice survival strategies. This month the drill will include the laminated map and the compass. After several training sessions, everybody should know exactly how to use a compass to orient themselves. They should also know how to use a map in conjunction with the compass to find their way from place to place. For the younger kids, making it into a game like hide-and-seek will make acquiring these new skills fun.

At this time, it is a good idea to pick out possible emergency evacuation routes. These should include places to meet if anyone gets lost, routes to nearby cities and towns, and places along the way that could offer help such as hospitals.

It can also be helpful to make note of any hotels that may be within a few hundred miles. In the event of a regional emergency, having this information handy can be of great value.

Month Twelve

"The time to repair the roof is when the sun is shining."
-John F. Kennedy

Congratulations! You have now reached the final month of the One Year Prepper Plan and have already acquired most of the basic supplies you will need to deal with either a short-term or long-term emergency. During this month you will be adding the last of the needed basic items. Also you may wish to include additional items as you continue your emergency preparations. More about including additional items is discussed in the next chapter.

Preparing a 72-Hour Kit

Now is the time for adding some essential items to your emergency preparedness kit. All supplies should be stored in a backpack that can be easily grabbed and taken with you should you need to leave in a hurry. Items to be added to this kit include:

- Two garbage bags per person.
- Emergency candles (in addition to candles added to long term storage supplies).
- Manual can opener.
- Vitamin C tablets (preferably chewable so you are not using valuable water just to take them).
- Forty dollars in cash.

Use this final month to take a look at the emergency clothing items you have previously packed for any children. If your children have already outgrown the items packed, replace them with clothes in the appropriate sizes. Make sure to check shoe sizes as well; children grow quickly and you may need to update the shoes, too. Take care to pack a sturdy pair that will protect feet from broken glass and other debris.

Additions to Long-Term Food Storage Supply

This month your mission is to add dried beans to your long-term food supply. Dried beans are inexpensive and keep for long periods of time. For a three month supply, you will need to add 10 pounds of dried beans per person. For a one year supply, pack 40 pounds of dried beans per person. Beans provide needed fiber and protein and can be eaten alone or added to soups and chilies. To use the dried beans, they will first need to soak in water for several hours to re-hydrate before they are ready to cook.

Additions to Shelter and Security Storage

This month you will be adding some final items to your shelter and security storage. Important items include:

- 20 emergency candles (this is just a starter supply; continue to add more over time to accumulate a large supply.).
- Batteries (Continually add to your battery supply taking care to check expiration dates. Rotate the supply as needed and use up the oldest ones for whatever you need them for, while replacing them

with fresh batteries for storage.).

This completes your basic list of supplies that will enable you to survive for up to a year during an emergency situation. These supplies are suitable for many different types of emergencies and situations.

Sources of Heat

Most of us rely on heat sources in our homes that use either electricity or gas, which is great if you have working utilities. In an emergency situation, you may not have access to working utilities, in which case you need to find another source of heat during the cold months. Summer emergencies can be miserable without air conditioning, but in most cases people can survive just fine as long as they remain properly hydrated. It is when the temperatures turn extremely cold that you could be in real danger. Here are some suggestions for possible heat sources during an emergency:

- Camping propane heater (Intended for outdoor use only, never use indoors!).
- Kerosene heater (May be used indoors ONLY with proper ventilation such as an open window.).
- Wood-burning stove.
- Wood-burning fireplace.
- Solar heating systems.

Determine which heating source will work best in your situation. After deciding, you will need to stock up on the appropriate fuel or firewood. Make sure to use safe and proper storage practices if using fuel sources.

Monthly Preparation Goal

Use this month to examine your insurance policies to ensure you have enough coverage. Many people are caught unprepared in an emergency. Check all policies including homeowners, renters, automobile and life insurance coverage.

Take into consideration such factors as if you were to have a fire, would your current policy cover all of the items you lost in addition to the cost of rebuilding the home? If you're a renter, would you have enough money to replace all of your personal belongings? For renters, your landlord will likely have a homeowner's policy to cover the loss of the house, but you will require renter's insurance in order to replace items such as furniture, clothing, electronics and other personal items.

If you are without a life insurance policy, now is the time to get one. Think of the hardship a death would cause your family if a breadwinner were to suddenly pass away. A death not only means loss of a loved one, but loss of income, plus many expenses such as funeral and burial costs. It is even beneficial to take out a small life insurance policy on children. Though no one ever wants to consider the unthinkable, especially when it comes to their children, things can happen and it is important to always be prepared. Not having life insurance when it is needed can make things extremely hard on all concerned, especially when coupled with dealing with another disaster or emergency.

Investing in long-term disability insurance is also a good call. Relying on the government for this is never a wise idea, and think of the hardship your family could be left with if a main breadwinner were suddenly unable to work and required long-term care as result of the disability.

Think of this month as being the time to get all of your ducks in a row in regards to your insurance policies.

Personalizing Your Prepper Plan

If you have followed all of the steps outlined in this book over the duration of one year's time, you will be well prepared and ahead of most other people should a disaster strike. With this said, you can still continue to work on your own preparation to make your stock suited to the specific needs of yourself and your family. Read on for more information about adding useful and helpful items to the ones you've already acquired.

Needs Specific to Location

Some areas are more prone to certain types of potential disasters than others, this means you may have additional needs specific to your location. Those in areas that routinely experience flooding or hurricanes may wish to include related items such as life jackets to their list, as well as an inflatable life raft. While it is still advisable to leave ahead of time to avoid a hurricane and associated flooding, if you are unable to leave or remain in a safe location, these items may enable you to safely evacuate your home in the event of an emergency where it is no longer safe to remain there.

Tailor your items to your individual location needs for whatever types of disasters you might face. For those in areas that frequently experience tornadoes, it may be wise to consider making an underground shelter, especially if you do not have a basement or some type of storm cellar. There is considerable expense in initially building a storm shelter; however, it is a worthwhile investment for keeping you and your loved ones safe during a life threatening weather event.

Areas with unusually harsh winters and excessive snowfalls should consider investing in items that may help you trek through the snow if needed. Snow shoes and skis are helpful in such climates, as well as a good supply of warm clothing. Stock up on blankets and other winter items that help provide light and warmth in the event of an emergency.

Consider Special Health Needs

If you or someone in your family has a health condition or impaired mobility issue that requires special attention, make accommodations to prepare for this condition during a long-term emergency. For example, in some cases this may include stocking up on an oxygen supply. Keep in mind that it is extremely important to follow safe handling and storage procedures because oxygen is extremely flammable. This also holds true for many other types of medical supplies. Be sure to store everything safely. Evaluate any special needs or concerns within your family and tailor your items to accommodate them.

Select Meal Options

We have focused on stocking up on basic supplies needed to make meals throughout the course of this guide. We've suggested items that are relatively inexpensive, readily available and appropriate for most households. There are also other convenience options you may wish to consider, such as MREs. This stands for Meals Ready to Eat and MREs are commonly used in the military as meals for those who are in combat. They are also now available for purchase in many survival supply stores and provide a large amount of needed calories in the form of a main dish, side dish, bread and dessert. The meals come with a flameless rations heater as well as handy plastic spoon inside.

MREs provide a good solution for the short-term and should usually not be eaten exclusively for more than three weeks' time. If you have no other option after three weeks, it is obviously better to continue eating the MREs as opposed to starving. Try using them as a treat in addition to the other food you have stocked. There are many different meal options to choose from and they will last in storage for many years.

Other items such as soups, stew, oatmeal, pastas, instant potatoes and rice, which require only the addition of water for preparation, can be found in many survival outlets and warehouse stores. Due to the dehydrated nature of the products, many of them have a shelf life of over twenty years. Food kits are also available and can be purchased in one month or even one year supplies.

No matter which food options you choose, it is advisable to try some of them to make sure you find them edible and appealing. In emergencies it's obvious that some food is better than no food regardless of taste, but the objective here is to be prepared for an emergency so that you can make your life as comfortable and normal as possible during the event. Items such as canned fruits and canned vegetables can also be used to supplement the meals, no matter which options are chosen. Make sure to include items that your family likes and will enjoy.

Adding Treats

Long term survival food options should also include treats, which can provide comfort during uncertain times. Along with all of the basics, include such tasty items like:

- Cookie, cake, and brownie mixes.
- Candies.
- Canned frosting.
- Hazelnut spread.
- Pancake mix.
- Chocolate chips, butterscotch chips, or peanut butter chips. Treats can go a long way to making long term emergency food supplies more interesting and appealing.

Don't Store Items You Don't Like and Won't Use

If you have come across food suggestions that you don't really care for throughout the course of this book, by all means leave those out of your food storage options. Simply find an appropriate substitute that works better for you and your family. Money spent on food that no one will eat, even during an emergency, is money wasted.

Beyond One Year - Staying Prepared

Protecting your home and all its inhabitants is an essential component for homeowners throughout the United States. While there are certain elements you should always follow to keep your home safe, such as always making sure doors and windows are locked; in order to ward off intruders, you must continually update your security measures and look for ways to further solidify your home.

Perhaps one of the most important elements when it comes to prepping your home against invaders is to continually seek out ways to increase your home security. While there are literally hundreds, if not thousands, of steps preppers can take to increase home security, the following are the most trusted and most common:

- Construct a reinforced fence around your property.
- Purchase effective body armor for yourself, and for every member of your family. While one hopes to never have to use body armor, it's one of those elements that is better to have and never need, than need and not have.
- A wide variety of self-defense weapons. Think outside of the box when it comes to objects you may use to protect your home and family.
- Ample ammunition supply for all weapons.

While the aforementioned are just a sample of basic storage and protection needs, the exact products you'll need are dependent on where you live and what threat level you wish to protect against.

Cash Reserve

It's easy to become caught up in methods and tools to protect your home, but one of the most essential elements for any survival prepper is to have an ample cash reserve stored within your property. When preparing your 72-hour emergency kit, gather more cash than you may believe is necessary. As a general rule of thumb, $1,000 in cash is the ideal amount to help secure basic needs should you be required to evacuate your home in a sudden emergency, such as an unplanned natural disaster.

A Variety of Bartering Items

While an excess of cash is an essential component for short-term survival, what happens when a natural disaster or some other threat prolongs civil unrest?

For example, the electrical grid within your city has been destroyed. As society delves back into pre-industrialized times, cash won't hold as much value as necessary items. A true survival prep kit should contain all, or at least some, of the following:

- Fire starting items, such as matches and lighters.
- Water purification tablets. In times when local water supplies have been polluted or if you're not able to obtain clean drinking water, water purification tablets can become a heavy bartering tool.

- Various OTC medications. Stock up on common pain relievers, antibacterial ointments, bandages and other simple medications.
- A variety of batteries. When the electrical grid fails, batteries will become a hotter commodity than $100 bills.
- Various Toiletry items. While not the most important out of this list, various toiletry items could become a luxury in cases of extreme civil unrest.
- Feminine hygiene and sanitary supplies.
- Long lasting candies.

Rotating Storage Inventory

It's essential when creating a survival kit to include items that feature long shelf lives; however, nothing can last forever. Therefore, as you add to your inventory keep track of each item and its expiration date. Seek out items that feature long expiration dates, which help prevent wasting money on products you never end up using.

Altering Inventory on Your Changing Needs

As life goes on, the items you need to carry out your daily duties will likely change. This is true for every member of your family. For example, when you started your survival kit your children may have been in diapers. Now, they may be in standard underwear. Therefore, your need for diapers and child-related gear is replaced by the need of adult-level supplies. Reevaluate your current inventory at least once per year to ensure its items meet the current needs for you and your family.

Continually Improve Your Survival Skills

The biggest mistake any survival prepper can make is relying too heavily on items and not your own skill level. The most successful preppers are those who continually increase their knowledge, physical strength and practical skill sets. Even if you don't plan on growing your own food, this is an essential skill to know in case the ease of driving to your grocery store is suddenly stripped from your life.

Other skills that are essential to master include:

- Food and water purification and preservation techniques. This includes knowing how to locate safe drinking water as well as how to procure food from gardening, hunting and fishing.
- Construction Skills. While you may not be expected to build a house, basic building and maintenance skills are essential for any prepper.
- Sewing. There may come a time where you must not only make your own clothing, but prolong the life of current clothes. Sewing, knitting, yarn making and other similar skills are vital for all preppers.
- Locating Shelter. In times where you and your family must escape urban centers, it's essential to know how to locate shelter, or how to build a shelter with items found in a rural environment.
- Weapons Training. Hopefully you'll never have to use these skills, but all preppers should know how to

properly fire, clean and load firearms.

- Playing an Instrument. Imagine a world without television or the Internet. Life as a prepper isn't always about seeking out ways to protect and feed your family. You must also know how to entertain yourself. Acoustic instruments are essential when modern society falls and entertainment options become limited.

Know that each of these skills can be cultivated over time. Strive to master at least one skill from this list every six months to a year. Seek out local educational courses and programs within your community. Most cities offer prepper-specific classes on the aforementioned skills and others.

Get Your Financial Life in Order

While you may not think getting your financial life in order as being a top priority when creating your survival prepper kit, not having any financial ties to an institution or other people frees up your options in case the worst case scenario were to happen. In order to accomplish this goal, strive to:

- Eliminate Consumer Debt. Focus on paying off your credit cards, auto loans and mortgage loan. No debt means you're able to save money and not be connected to any financial institution.
- Save up enough money to equal six months of income.
- Create an effective retirement plan.

* * *

When the dreaded economic downswing occurs, you don't want to have to focus on spending all your money on your debt or mortgage payments. In case you lose your employment due to an economic crisis, being debt free allows you to use all your saved money on your family without having to worry about being kicked out of your home or having your cars repossessed due to non-payment.

A Lifetime of Preparation

One of the most important elements to remember, above everything else in this article, is to realize survival preparation lasts a lifetime. Preparing for a major disaster requires continual concentration and involvement. Focus on improving your survival techniques by increasing your self-reliance and focusing on what you and your family require in case our civilization finally takes a hit. While this can be a confusing start, the One Year Prepper Plan is an essential start to this lifelong journey.